Two Lectures

Leftovers: *A Care Package*

William Stafford

From Anne to Marianne: *Some Women in American Poetry*

Josephine Jacobsen

Library of Congress

Washington

1973

Library of Congress Cataloging in Publication Data
Main entry under title:
Two lectures.

The lecture by W. Stafford was delivered at the Library of Congress on May 3, 1971; the one by J. Jacobsen on May 1, 1972.
Includes bibliographical references.
1. United States. Library of Congress. Poetry Office. 2. Women as poets. 3. American poetry—History and criticism. I. Stafford, William Edgar, 1914–   Leftovers. 1973. II. Jacobsen, Josephine. From Anne to Marianne. 1973. III. United States. Library of Congress. IV. Title. Leftovers. V. Title: From Anne to Marianne.
Z733.U58T9   811'.009   72–13401

ISBN 0–8444–0049–1

For sale by the Superintendent of Documents, U.S. Government Printing Office, Washington, D.C. 20402 - Price: 35 cents domestic postpaid, or 25 cents GPO Bookstore Stock Number 3016–00019

Contents

Acknowledgments

William Stafford served as Consultant in Poetry in English at the Library of Congress, 1970–71, and presented this lecture at the Library on May 3, 1971.

Leftovers: *A Care Package*

LET ME REMIND YOU of things around us now, not things apparent by sound or sight or any physical sense, but things imminent and real. I don't mean spiritual beings, as in Milton's "Millions of spiritual creatures walk the earth,/Unseen, both when we wake and when we sleep," nor do I mean ultra-high frequency waves. I mean real in the sense of potential, or simply faint and *unrealized.* Among these things are such as stir us sometimes in the arts and then get lost in our formulations, our inadequate ways of communicating.

Some such thought made me decide, in planning for this occasion, to remind myself to be alert, to be aware of the nowness of things—the feel of the day, the temperature, the kind of room, the people, what they said. This attempt to be aware springs from an opinion, a fear, maybe a superstition about art: any time we adopt a stance that induces the analytical feeling about art we may be subverting what art lives by. This superstition makes me jumpy about giving a talk as part of the job of being poetry consultant. My impulse is to make this talk strange and jumpy.

We in the Poetry Office at the Library often find ourselves in the presence of something imminent and real, but not quickly identifiable, when we face a seemingly simple question. Sometimes this question comes on first encounter; sometimes it comes later, even as a guilty-sounding aside late in the evening at a party where acquaintance has been built up enough to afford the assumption of goodwill. The question implies a readiness to be secret and forgiving: "What does the Poetry Office really do?"

The Library administration has supplied us with an explicit and impressive list of functions, and I can usually remember enough of them to use in response, so as to sound useful and frank, and *engaged,* like other workers. Possessed of such a list, why do I almost always feel somehow guilty? Why does a recital of the functions leave me and the questioner looking baffled? There is some leftover, or residue, or essence not identified, apparently.

On that list of functions, all relate to the interest and concern of the Library, and once that relation is assumed it is easy to run through several jobs: 1) to maintain contact with literary people; 2) to recommend writers to be recorded; 3) to give some lectures or readings; 4) to advise on programs and activities; 5) to write a literary essay; and 6) to find other ways to help.

Those functions—or at least some of them—are definite enough. In our office we can make an effort to accomplish every one, to some degree. We try. We can even measure our accomplishment, and report. Something in the nature of the job, however, makes us aware that the administration, the people in other offices, the visitors who come to see us, the audiences at the literary programs, and the people who write to us all feel a pause amidst the explicit interchange. There is something else. Maybe every human activity has this extra dimension, some kind of deeper element. Our office happens to encounter this questioning, this need, to a perceptible degree in a lasting way. Early in my time here I made a resolve to wait, to listen, to discover.

This report relates to that endeavor after an inexplicable leftover or residue. My assumption is that the actual, if encountered rightly, can teach and accumulate and resonate with itself to become significant. Some kinds of work, and some kinds of life, can unfold from experience as it goes along. I want to attempt a report on the Poetry Office as that kind of unreeling discovery.

The first formal visit to our office last fall may serve to identify procedure and one kind of result. Elliott Coleman of Johns Hopkins brought Edward Brathwaite of Jamaica for a session to record Brathwaite's poems for the Library archives. I put my camera in an inconspicuous bag, reminded myself to be alert and receptive, and went down to meet the two of them in a way that became the pattern for such encounters.

The work of both visitors was known to me ("Maintain contact with literary people"). Elliott Coleman shows up in the picture taken that day: gray hair, steady eyes. To me, he is a symbol of literary accomplishment over the years, an influence on student generations in his writing program. He had arranged for the recording session by his friend Edward Brathwaite, whose British accent revealed his education. His dark skin and hair and dress marked his Jamaica background, and his poems—with drum rhythms and African words occasionally—showed his intention to relate his art to the culture of that African part of his background. My picture of him shows an alert stance on the balcony of the Library toward the Capitol; in one pose his dark glasses reflect the traffic on First Street.

In our office, when we look at those pictures and think of that day, we sense a reaching, a communication about a sustained endeavor. I do not know how to add that day's essence to the explicit list of functions for our office. But the extra, the leftover, that occurs to me is this: Mr. Coleman and Mr. Brathwaite did not establish any regular, or competitive, or purposeful contact that day. No one of us continued the visit beyond what we wanted, what we enjoyed. The unfolding of the visit in terms of its own liveliness remains with me, as an example of what was to follow in other visits in which a seeker would come, meet us, view the arrangements, and then look at us on leaving: What does the Poetry Office do?

Recklessly, I make a lunge for a leftover from that day, something faint, that may not link at all, from this distance:

Three Looks Out of a Window

1.

Someone Went By

Someone went by in the alley
singing. The dogs trained their
ears and followed around a whole
arc of attention. In this air shell
each hermit carries his home.

We never knew who it was.

2.

Up in the Hills

Each place out of the wind has a name
so swift it escapes your lips when you
enter. You say it like the password God
already knows at His altar. But if
the spirit is wrong, then no matter how clear,
the word can't work. You go into each room
like that, naming it, humble: it sorts
itself out like the next look of your face.
Each room in the hills, they say,
belongs right where it is.

3.

LONESOME

If you care, come by. We have
this place no one but a traveler sees.
And the only real traveler in a year
is the one in the leaves, inside the bundle
of leaves: the year itself. It says farewell
a million times, each time forever.

It happened that our next visitor was also from abroad, from India—Mr. Shrikant Varma. He came introduced by someone from the USIA, but not in terms of an official introduction: the USIA person was himself a poet and had become friends with Mr. Varma while traveling. We listened to this new visitor, who brought us a gift, a book in that graceful language of loops and lines, a book we hold but cannot read. He and I had lunch at the Supreme Court Building. Then we sat on the grass and talked and looked at the people strolling around the Capitol grounds ("Maintain contact with literary people"). I cannot say that our talk linked firmly to those listed functions of my job. That talk was a leftover. Mr. Varma told me that Washington is one of the best capitals he had seen. He was on the way to Iowa, to study with writers from many parts of the world. He told me of his work, newspaper work, in India. He took poetry very seriously; he knew American literature. The people walking on the Capitol grounds became part of a richer scene, because of Shrikant Varma. In my picture, taken at a reception that evening, he is looking mildly to one side. I remember that just after the camera snapped someone reached over my eyes with both hands and said, "Guess who?" It was a guest at the party, an old friend, excited and talkative. I wonder what Mr. Varma thought of that swirl there.

Here is a leftover from that encounter:

Compliments to a Visitor

You raised your eyebrows at the right
time when we talked and I could not phrase
the question. How could anyone
know how important that was? All afternoon
you had a way you looked out

and accepted the sun or the rain. When
the visit was over you walked slowly, but
did not look back. I liked that, and
the certain place you perched on the desk,
and that little trick of the foot holding
the whole world still when it was late
and we had almost cornered an idea.

Other visitors from abroad have come, each with a new gift for us. Something of what they brought must be woven into all that follows, but I want to make an intentional turn to another kind of leftover, this time what resulted from visitors from here at home.

Of all the experiences this year at the Poetry Office, the encounters with persons who came for conferences have been the biggest surprise and the most frequent rewards. Many people who seek an encounter either are writers themselves or represent someone who writes. And almost invariably the person is apologetic, for what is sought appears to be approval or instruction, or both; in any case, something awkward to solicit. But here is where the surprise comes: not one such visitor has failed to bring significant insights and gains to our office. I think I glimpse a truth hard to say, something that even the visitors might deny: what they really bring is a talisman or reward from a search that has already succeeded. From these people I learn that the way we phrase our goals and accomplishments in the arts fails to identify rightly the real endeavor. Lest I appear to be evading, I must bring forward a particular, but there is a reason to be cautious, for I do not want to identify any one of these persons whose writings have all led to the claim that there is a significant accomplishment even in the attempting of the arts. But I can give an example.

One man was in economics; he had worked 15 years or so in an office of international trade. He consulted us because he was trying to bring into words a complex feeling he had about the goals of his life and of his children's lives. He felt that our kind of culture was sweeping his children into competitive habits, that the more important possibilities in their lives were being slighted by the daily-ness of existence. There have been a number of such people in our office, people whose lives are steady and successful, but whose impulses have led them aside, even into poetry.

Often these seekers put their comments or questions into predictable forms, but I do not believe the real issues are what those predictable formulations seem to assume. In assessing the leftovers from this type of visitor I have tried out and abandoned a number of versions, all of them leading toward somewhat different implications. I will settle for this one formulation, intended to indicate just a possibility for the direction a discussion can go: the appeal may be, "Is my manuscript any good?" Or more helpfully put, the question may be, "How can my manuscript be corrected?"

Not from my own analysis, but as a result of considering leftovers from many such encounters, I offer, not an answer, but a response. Once a person enters the kind of sustained relation between himself and what occurs to him in language, the idea of correcting the result is not an adequate idea. The Poetry Office has to do with manuscripts that cannot be corrected toward quality. What a person is asking, once he enters the area of art, is reverberation, or human response—*company*. And that need is legitimate. A helpful reentry into the creative process, however, is something that another person cannot do for the seeker. True, many persons do suggest or "correct," but any such simple assumption of another's role—especially when well intentioned and serious—is immediately a violation of what art is all about.

Again and again at the Poetry Office we have found that these visits become mutually helpful. Always, though, the basis of the gain is some kind of human encountering that does not have to do with an assessment of accomplishment in the terms of negotiability on the market or "worth" in the community.

A leftover from this kind of relation is "Our Story":

After the ink drink, off
over the miles of white,
nose down, rooting its life
all the way from the Renaissance
or before and bound silently
for Hope's home, God's home, the end,

So goes the pen, to tell
the whole story, up through
the hand and arm into
a code on the thread of time,

or to stare into the earth,
find something the boarhound passed,
an animal that dodged the heather
and left no track: man.

He is here somewhere today,
frightened among us, held
prisoner, doubled back
from the cliff again. Tomorrow,
rested, he has a chance once more—

After the ink drink, off
over the miles of white,
nose down, rooting for life
all the way from the Renaissance
or before and bound silently
for Hope's home, God's home, the end.

In passing, it occurs to me to mention a kind of visitor we did not have, a kind that an outsider might assume would be around. I mean a person who questions not the quality of what he is doing but the *use* of it. Few encounters at the Poetry Office brought this question—so looming a question for many in society—into focus. I can think of several reasons for this lack. One is that a whole sector of poets have *a priori* convictions: they are writing to bring about ends they have already identified as important. These writers are technicians of language, yoking it to political and social ends, or they are intense partisans of persons or movements that proclaim their own importance. Such people seldom visit the Poetry Office, at least for reasons connected with their concern about poetry. And I think these persons are right in neglecting us on this score, for the whole tendency of art as I have been presenting it is different from the project these committed people have in mind.

And another group fail to raise the issue of the use of poetry—those who are so innocent that they think anything they happen to like is important. I love these people and want to include my innocent self among them.

Now let me try for that extra function of the Poetry Office, that element we sense as a leftover in any outline of work. No narrative now, no asides—a summary.

The Poetry Office concerns itself with an activity that cannot be identified by usual designations, not by intention or worldly result, but by feeling. The activity comes about by willingly entering an area of possible encounter. The immediacy of each encounter is the guide for sequential moves. To have in mind patterns other than those discovered by way of immediate experience is to violate the process being used. Some people cannot lend themselves in a sustained way to such art activity. Even some writers give it up. They get lost.

Because I do not know whether the Poetry Office can or should be identified in such terms, justifying itself but denying an objective other than the allowing of a result that may derive from a way of living, I turn to a few poems that have resulted from this way of life. Maybe the poems can bear the burden of their own justification, and as they grow from the process I have identified, they may pertain to a judgment at this time of casting back.

Stories to Live in the World With

1.

A long rope of gray smoke was
coming out of the ground. I went
nearer and looked at it sideways.
I think there was a cave, and some people
were in a room by a fire in the earth.
One of them thought of a person like me
coming near but never quite coming in
to know them.

2.

Once a man killed another, to rob him,
but found nothing, except that lying
there by a rock was a very sharp,
glittering little knife. The murderer
took the knife home and put it beside
his bed, and in the night he woke
and the knife was gone. But there was
no way for a person to get in to take the knife.

The man went to a wise old woman.
When she heard the story, she began to laugh.

The man got mad. He yelled at the woman
to tell why she was laughing. She looked
at him carefully, with her eyes squinted
as if she looked at the sun. "Can't you
guess what happened?" she asked.

The man didn't want to be dumb; so
he thought and thought. "Maybe the knife
was so sharp that it fell on the ground
and just cut its way deeper and deeper and
got away." The woman squinted some more.
She shook her head. "You learned that from
a story. No, I will tell you why you
thought the knife was gone and why
you came here to ask me about it:
you are dead."

Then the man noticed that he didn't
have any shadow. He went out and
looked around: nothing had any shadow.
He began to squint up his eyes, it was
all so bright. And wherever he looked
there were sharp little knives.

This is a true story. He really was dead.
My mother told us about it. She told us
never to kill or rob.

3.

At a little pond in the woods
I decided: this is the center of my life.
I threw a big stick far out, to be
all the burdens from earlier years.
Ever since, I have been walking
lightly, looking around, out of the woods.

Two more I want to cite are from sojourners in the office. The first is by the former consultant I most easily understand from congeniality and sympathy, Reed Whittemore.

The Party

They served tea in the sandpile, together with
Mudpies baked on the sidewalk.
After tea
The youngest said that he had had a good dinner,
The oldest dressed for a dance,
And they sallied forth together with watering pots
To moisten a rusted fire truck on account of it
Might rain.

I watched from my study,
Thought of my part in these contributions to world
Gaiety, and resolved
That the very least acknowledgment I could make
Would be to join them;
so we
All took our watering pots (filled with pies)
And poured tea on our dog. Then I kissed the children
And told them that when they grew up we would have
Real tea parties.
"That did be fun!" the youngest shouted, and ate pies
With wild surmise.

Another example is from the work of Josephine Jacobsen, who comes to the office next fall:

The Stranger and Corrigan

I asked Corrigan about the man, alone at the wood's edge,
Who stood in shadow; the motionless stranger,
He did not stir or speak, and he bore in his face and eyes
The marks perhaps of terrible cold and certainly hunger.

I had come through the journey alive, and into the field
And the sun would have warmed the dead and made them answer;
And I saw the way he stood, and his coat, and hands.
A stranger returned from this trip is more close than a brother.

So I spoke the word of the way, and he answered once;
But he never moved or came through the windy flowers.
And I said to Corrigan, "He is one of them
But he will not smile or speak—only watches the mowers.

"The field will be gone," I said, "while he stands and looks—
Tell him I am one—though I went, it is true, in summer."
But Corrigan would not question him and the mowers moved
Bright in the glitter of grasses, toward the newcomer.

"Bitter and strange, I agree, in summer as in winter;
But different in winter. Also," Corrigan said,
"Tell me: when you went, and lived, and returned—
Did you travel alone, and without bread?"

I like the strangeness of this poem and can't help feeling that it bodes well for the continued strangeness of a job I have found wonderfully congenial, a job I have tried to identify, in an odd way, with leftovers. Josephine Jacobsen, stranger: come to the office; take up this effort; look people in the eye who ask you, casually, or late after a party, when even the most cautious can assume goodwill: "What does the Poetry Office do?"

Acknowledgments

Josephine Jacobsen, the 1971–73 Consultant in Poetry in English, delivered this lecture at the Library of Congress on May 1, 1972.

From Anne to Marianne:
Some Women in American Poetry

THE TITLE OF THIS TALK was selected with care. Few things are more boring than lists, and what I want to talk about in this brief time is not a chronological survey of the women poets of America. I want to look at the atmosphere in which they worked, to attempt to understand a little of its pressures and permissions; and I hope that in some mysterious way I may manage to combine elements of the involved and of the objective. As an American woman poet, I can scarcely fail to be involved, but it is the poetry, not the nationality or the sex, which finally matters. In this whole question, sentimentality and exhortation are equally lethal, and there is a delicate balance between ignoring the question of power and powerlessness, and making social and human problems, instead of the poetry, the center of attention.

The arts have a frequently quarrelsome, but always close, relationship. The Walters Art Gallery is currently exhibiting a show interestingly called "Old Mistresses," this being not a sort of Nell Gwynn exploration, but a commentary on the ease with which we automatically accept the classification Old Masters. What some of the passages in the Walters *Bulletin* tell us is so closely related to the history of American women who have practiced another art form, that of poetry, that I must quote it. The *Bulletin* itself quotes an influential book of etiquette of the period of Mary Cassatt, which sums up the desirable attitude for women who are in danger of becoming involved in the arts:

> To be able to do a great many things tolerably well, is of infinitely more value to a woman, than to be able to excel in any one. By the former, she may render herself generally useful; by the latter, she may dazzle for an hour. . . . So far as cleverness, learning, and knowledge are conducive to a woman's moral excellence, they are therefore desirable, and no further. All that would occupy her mind to the exclusion of better things, all that would involve her in the mazes of flattery and admiration, [mazes of course

untrod by masculine foot] all that would tend to draw away her thoughts from others and fix them on herself, ought to be avoided as an evil to her, however brilliant or attractive it may be in itself.[1]

The Walters' voice adds: "Adopting this philosophy would automatically prevent a woman, married or single, from developing a serious commitment to any profession." And it notes that after Mary Cassatt defied her father's prohibition, went to Europe, and by a tremendous struggle established herself as a serious painter—and incidentally supported herself as such—the denouement was characteristically discouraging:

> Although Cassatt's father had been strictly against her sojourn in Europe, shortly after she settled in Paris he forgot his misgivings and brought the entire family to live with her.

The *Bulletin* adds that from then on she ran the household, took her invalid mother on health trips, nursed her ailing sister, and superintended the family's numerous moves, without it having seemed to occur to anyone that this was making any illegitimate inroads on her professional work or her creative energy.

This has a sadly familiar ring. Anne Bradstreet, the only poet of creative stature with the exception of Edward Taylor in a hundred years of American literature, was well aware of the reaction to her writing poetry at all. She wrote, with considerable bluntness, in "The Prologue":

> I am obnoxious to each carping tongue
> Who says my hand a needle better fits,
> A poet's pen all scorn I should thus wrong,
> For such despite they cast on female wits:
> If what I do prove well, it won't advance,
> They'll say it's stol'n, or else it was by chance.

That is an undermining atmosphere. This reaction, of course, was not entirely limited to women. In *100 American Poems* Selden Rodman quotes a letter which Herman Melville's wife wrote to her mother in 1859: "Herman has taken to writing poetry. You need not tell anyone for you know how such things get around." The distinction, however, remains in the fact that men were not supposed to write poetry because it was unsuitable, since they had things of authority and importance to do. Women were not supposed to write poetry because buttons would stay missing and meals be late, not to mention the degradation of morals.

It is simply impossible, as it is in the case of all highly subjective and emotional issues, to say with any certainty what effect the problems and harassments actually traceable to Anne Bradstreet's femininity had on her work, chilling and shrinking it: the overwhelming atmosphere of incredulity and misprision; the physical strains of a woman's life in what she described as "the savage wilderness of America," where she bore eight children and watched the deaths of three small grandchildren, two little girls aged a year and a half, and three years and seven months, and a little boy who lived a month and a day. Surrounded by so much death, the old struggle to accept came through:

> But plants new set to be eradicate,
> And buds new blown to have so short a date,
> Is by His hand alone that guides nature and fate.

And then the more desolate:

> I knew she was but as a withering flower,
> That's here today, perhaps gone in an hour;
> Like as a bubble, or the brittle glass,
> Or like a shadow turning as it was.
> More fool then I to look on that was lent
> As if mine own, when thus impermanent.

There is a Herrick-like echo in those lines.

In addition to the mental climate peculiar to women, there was the total lack of immediate contact with any world of letters. Kenneth Silverman, speaking in *Colonial American Poetry* of the appalling doggerel turned out, points up this barrenness:

> . . . although there was a great volume of verse produced in the colonies, there never was a literary class. In a century and a half of their existence, the colonies supported not one professional imaginative writer.[2]

It is amazing what a death-grip the concept of genteel composition had. With a raw and magnificent continent surrounding them, with melodrama, conquest, cruelty, courage, and despair all around them, the colonial poets struggled to simulate the ambiance of a salon. Silverman comments:

The jarring effect of much eighteenth-century colonial verse, the reader's sense that the poet has not responded appropriately to the occasion, is the upshot of training a refined and chaste diction on the affairs of unformed towns and wilderness outposts.[3]

The women writing poetry in this entire period do seem to have been genuinely and often passionately involved in writing as a form of good works. It is a sobering instruction to see how poorly verse, widely acclaimed for its propaganda value in the interest of excellent causes, has withstood the test of time. Actually, the case for polemical poetry is put grandiloquently, but rather movingly, in Samuel Kettell's early *Specimens of American Poetry:*

. . . when the aim of the aggressor is at the very heart of civil liberty, the dwellers in the shades of the Academy, and even the loiterers in the laurel groves of the Muses have never been the last to repel the advances of the invader.

That is the principle. The practice has been less impressive. There was an enormous amount of poetry written by women, attacking current evils: slavery, alcoholism, the oppression of the working classes, the oppression of the Indian. Some of it, in its day, did quite probably influence other human beings and so, in some minute degree, succeed in its author's purpose. As poetry, it left scarcely a wrack behind. Lydia Huntley Sigourney wrote a just, and spirited, and far from untalented poem called "The Indian's Welcome to the Pilgrim Fathers." But not even our present high concern with the reevaluation of the confrontations between Indians and settlers has served to revive interest in it. In our day there are poems by Josephine Miles, Denise Levertov, and Adrienne Rich good enough to give the lie to the generalization that poetry with an object is, *per se,* bad poetry; but the winnowing-out has been, in the long view, usually pitiless to the poetry of polemics.

Although the poetry of colonial America was very bad indeed, its content does tell us a number of things. What were the chief elements in the attitudes of American women poets in the long desert stretching between Anne Bradstreet and Emily Dickinson? The chief elements—and this statement is less provocative than realistic—were those one might expect from a body of literate, highly privileged slaves. In general, life is seen as something to be endured; emotion as something foredoomed; death as a release, even for the young. Much of the poetry of any force deals with the idea of emotional escape—as indeed does so much of the later poetry of Emily Dickinson. In a period when, out of a family of 14 or 15 children, five or six might well die in infancy or early childhood, death as an omnipresent reality was a towering presence. The constants in the lives of women poets in the first hundred and fifty years on this continent were endurance, faith (often less as a conviction than as a desperate refuge), and a courage that was less ardent than fatalistic. When Louise Imogen Guiney, an uneven but much underrated poet, later wrote in "The Kings,"

> "The terrible Kings are on me,
> . . . .
> Mind's Doubt and Bodily Pain,
> And pallid Thirst of the Spirit
> That is kin to the other twain, . . ."

she was echoing her predecessors. Expressed agnosticism, in a woman, would have been as unseemly (and this is the point) as a talent for wrestling; so that whatever agonies of doubt the events of their lives might induce must be met and vanquished—or not—in secret.

It would be naive in the extreme to imagine that women poets accepted the innate superiority of men as mentors or artists without inner questioning, but for the most part, any overt caviling took the form of the lightest of mockery. I want to read two brief verses, each of which is typical of a sort of graceful disillusionment and more than typical of its period. Hannah Parker Kimball's "One Way of Trusting":

> Not trust you, dear? Nay, 't is not true.
>   As sailors trust the shifting sea
> From day to day, so I trust you.
>   They know how smooth the sea can be;
> And well they know its treachery
>   When tempests blow; yet forth they thrust
> Their ships, as in security.
>   They trust it, dear, because they must.

And Charlotte Perkins Stetson relieved her feelings after encountering the resistance of a male to the very notion of change, no matter what improvement it involved. "A Conservative":

The garden beds I wandered by
  One bright and cheerful morn,
When I found a new-fledged butterfly,
  A-sitting on a thorn,
A black and crimson butterfly,
  All doleful and forlorn.

. . . . . .

Cried he, "My legs are thin and few
  Where once I had a swarm!
Soft fuzzy fur—a joy to view—
  Once kept my body warm,
Before these flapping wing-things grew,
  To hamper and deform!"

At that outrageous bug I shot
  The fury of mine eye;
Said I, in scorn all burning hot,
  In rage and anger high,
"You ignominious idiot!
  Those wings are made to fly!"

"I do not want to fly," said he,
  "I only want to squirm!"
And he drooped his wings dejectedly,
  But still his voice was firm:
"I do not want to be a fly!
  I want to be a worm!"

It is a gentle stricture.

I may interpolate here that there has been a strong implication by gentlemen reviewers that there is something intrinsically humorous and definitive, in the worst sense, about the three-name woman poet. And indeed, a great number of the triple-threat ladies have been very, very bad. If, however, the poetic stature of Ralph Waldo Emerson, Edgar Allan Poe, Edwin Arlington Robinson, Gerard Manley Hopkins, or William Butler Yeats, for example, has been pegged to the number of their employed names, I have not observed it.

And it is only fair to admit that, if most early American poetry written by women was little better than refined doggerel, one can usually suffer similar shock from their male counterparts. One reads a woman's ode to General Washington and encounters the following lines:

> And Echo no longer is plaintively mourning,
> But laughs and is jocund as we,
> And the turtle-eyed nymphs, to their cots all returning,
> Carve Washington on every tree.

It takes one a minute to realize that the turtle-eyed nymphs returning to their cots do not represent a sort of reptilian dormitory, but doves. But then one encounters a patriotic poem of exhortation by the author of "Dixie," Albert Pike, as he adjures his fellow Confederates,

> Strong as lions, swift as eagles,
> Back to their kennels hunt these beagles!

I do think the picture of a combination of lions and eagles attacking a group of beagles seems unfair.

In the long line that stretches from the bleak poetic environment of Anne Bradstreet to the complex surroundings of Marianne Moore, it is interesting, I think, to note certain resemblances between two of the finest American poets: Miss Moore herself and Emily Dickinson. Each was a spinster. Each lived uninvolved in the physical and emotional relationships which alter the daily circumstances of a wife or mother. Each had a fine quiddity which went its own way, owing nothing to the current poetic fashion. Marianne Moore, of course, lived a life enormously enriched by contacts with her peers, by access to other milieux, by her freedom from the rigid expectations of contemporaries. Emily Dickinson had a close kinship with her predecessors not only in her preoccupation with death, which Conrad Aiken so rightly noted, but in that same sense of suffocation, in the passionate need for an emotional breakthrough, which gives her work so many of its images. Three very brief Dickinson poems make, I think, an entire emotional history. I want to read them in sequence, without comment.[4]

> What Soft—Cherubic Creatures—
> These Gentlewomen are—

One would as soon assault a Plush—
Or violate a Star—

Such Dimity Convictions—
A Horror so refined
Of freckled Human Nature—
Of Deity—ashamed—

It's such a common—Glory—
A Fisherman's—Degree—
Redemption—Brittle Lady—
Be so—ashamed of Thee—

And the next:

Exultation is the going
Of an inland soul to sea,
Past the houses—past the headlands—
Into deep Eternity—

Bred as we, among the mountains,
Can the sailor understand
The divine intoxication
Of the first league out from land?

And the last:

How many times these low feet staggered—
Only the soldered mouth can tell—
Try—can you stir the awful rivet—
Try—can you lift the hasps of steel!

Stroke the cool forehead—hot so often—
Lift—if you care—the listless hair—
Handle the adamantine fingers
Never a thimble—more—shall wear—

Buzz the dull flies—on the chamber window—
Brave—shines the sun through the freckled pane—
Fearless—the cobweb swings from the ceiling—
Indolent Housewife—in Daisies—lain!

So little did Moore or Dickinson draw the matter of their poems from events and circumstantial changes in their own lives. Dickinson's came from within. Moore's, most of the time, from reading—reading of the odd, the particular, the out-of-the-way, the intricate. The overwhelming majority of her poems were drawn from bits of information which, like a sublime packrat, she carried off, only to return in their place a masterly poem. There has been much recent discussion of *attention* as prayer, and William Stafford has discussed *poetry* as *attention*. Observation, raised to a certain degree, is a kind of love. Marianne Moore is the empress of observation. This is a passage from the book which William Mueller and I wrote on Samuel Beckett—we speak of Beckett's quality as poet:

> There is the poetry in which the observation is of such passionate fidelity . . . [that its intensity of] vision celebrates the nature of the thing observed, be that nature what it may. . . . In this intensification . . . the things of . . . poetry are seen by that peculiar clarity in which trees, flowers, a cat on green grass will stand in the light just before a thunderstorm, when the grass seems itself to give off light and the flowers to be carved on the air. The poetry consists . . . in the intensification of the thing itself.[5]

In the wonderful, casual phrase, Miss Moore *paid* attention, and the things to which she paid it rewarded her: the jerboa, the swan, a steeple-jack, a scalpel, the weasel, steam rollers, mongooses, snails, racehorses, steel, granite, giraffes, baseball, and their qualities and uses. Her attention ran below the surface: how yarn is dyed, how the structure of a wing functions, how a steeple is gilded, how an octopus kills its prey with "concentric, crushing rigor." On and on. A man's eye for the accurate detail, Anne Bradstreet's detractors would have said. But this sort of eye is notably shared by May Swenson and by Elizabeth Bishop.

The liberation by art precedes the liberation by circumstance. By the time in which an American woman, Harriet Monroe, was establishing a magazine, *Poetry*, which was to become perhaps the world's leading journal of poetry, the entire paralyzing structure of the attitude toward women writers had begun to show cracks, and then gaps. In the first half of this century, no one could argue that Elinor Wylie or Edna St. Vincent Millay was forced into passive attitudes in the face of a masculine world. Yet, in the technical sense, they were still sports, and their response to life was often a sort of ricochet of their reaction to a masculine world. Millay, in particular, showed clearly a sort of midway struggle in the process of self-identification. A new note is sounded. This is not one of her best poems, but it is the perfect illustration of her simultaneous attack and insecurity.

I, being born a woman and distressed
By all the needs and notions of my kind,
Am urged by your propinquity to find
Your person fair, and feel a certain zest
To bear your body's weight upon my breast:
So subtly is the fume of life designed,
To clarify the pulse and cloud the mind,
And leave me once again undone, possessed.

Think not for this, however, the poor treason
Of my stout blood against my staggering brain,
I shall remember you with love, or season
My scorn with pity,—let me make it plain:
I find this frenzy insufficient reason
For conversation when we meet again.

That's a far cry, but it still assumes "the needs and notions" of a woman to be her Achilles heel. The later *Conversation At Midnight* examines the conversation of six men, without hostility and with considerable empathy. It is noticeable that the only woman present is the observant spirit of Vincent, who notoriously preferred masculine company. Miss Millay had the misfortune to be too often remembered by the tag-lines of her light verse, her shining palaces built on the sands and her candle flaming at each end. Her reputation is now in that trough between the adulation of her work when it was in vogue and the steady respect I believe it will be entitled to, in its finest forms. I notice that Karl Shapiro has spoken of returning to his "schoolboy love Millay" and being enchanted all over again.

What of the women poets of the present? Without for a moment blinking the fact that the scales are still heavily loaded in the world of everyday activity, it would be impossible, I think, to maintain the claim that women poets today have any limitation imposed upon their concepts, or the expression of those concepts. However, influences can be extremely subtle, and yet strong. Since the vast majority of women do not actually follow as many styles of life, move about in their environments in just the same way, experience the same physical and economic pressures as do men—to that extent, the material which comes naturally to their hand is more limited. A woman who is not, in the popular imagination, responsible for the economic support of a large family, a woman who is not going to be instructed to drop a bomb or wield a bayonet, is having, for better or worse, her separate experience. How much this will change is here beyond the point. The fact is that, as Dickinson was able to pour a passionate emotional life into the tiny mold of her circumstances, it has been demonstrated again and again that when it comes to making bricks without straw, women have possessed an infinite and mysterious skill. More and more straw becomes available. The poetry of women today does not show an overwhelming satisfaction with the quality of that straw. The poetry of Mona Van Duyn, Gwendolyn Brooks, Isabella Gardner, Adrienne Rich, Anne Sexton, Carolyn Kizer, is racked by the pressures and tensions of their wider experience. Julia Randall is one of the few who, more and more, show a quality of underlying radiance—a sort of receptive joy under the full recognition of suffering and even horror. There is a beautiful poem by Muriel Rukeyser which illustrates the sort of radiance of which I am speaking. It's called "This Place in the Ways."

Having come to this place
I set out once again
On the dark and marvelous way
From where I began:
Belief in the love of the world,
Woman, spirit, and man.

Having failed in all things
I enter a new age
Seeing the old ways as toys,
The houses of a stage
Painted and long forgot;
And I find love and rage.

Rage for the world as it is
But for what it may be
More love now than last year.
And always less self-pity

Since I know in a clearer light
The strength of the mystery.

And at this place in the ways
I wait for song,
My poem-hand still, on the paper,
All night long.
Poems in throat and hand, asleep,
And my storm beating strong!

I believe that the incoming tide of good poetry by American women is going to expand and deepen, not steadily—poetry never works in that way—but erratically. It is not any security on the part of women which is going to cause this to happen. Poetry has small traffic with security. What *will* contribute is the sense of the freedom, and hence power, of the individual woman (if the realization of that status for women does not tragically coincide with the diminution of all of us, men and women alike)—the right of the human being who is a woman to act, and react, *as* an individual, as the sort of human creature she is, without being first and most important judged within the context of that constricting niche to which society has assigned her.

William Jay Smith quotes Louise Bogan in his fine lecture *A Woman's Words*: ". . . the woman poet has her singular role and precious destiny." In a preface I wrote some years ago to *Lyrics of Three Women* (one of whom was Washington's May Sullivan), I said of the best women poets: "They extract, from the husk; they mine the lode for what it yields, and learn, as they do it." Like Roethke, they learn by going where they have to go.

Power is related to energy, and poetry is energy. The power to which poetry is allied is not political or financial power, but moral, physical, and intellectual power. Bad things, such as war, suffering, and competition under harsh conditions, often produce magnificent by-products such as courage, compassion, and skilled responsibility—what Hopkins called "the achieve of, the mastery of the thing." Not only have women not had physical power analogous to that of men, it must be remembered that until this century they never had the power delegated through the machine—electricity, the automobile, the household robots which remove much of the drudgery—and that in the past, where they had native intellectual and artistic power, it was all too often cut off from implementation. No group oppressed—and it is possible to speak of oppression, since the denial to any individual of the power within her human potential is certainly the earmark of oppression—no group oppressed ever frees itself or flowers without the traces of that oppression, without a shrillness, an aggressiveness, an infatuation with their own idiosyncracies, as though anything, to be interesting or valid, had only to belong to them. I think much of the extravagantly confessional kind of poetry written by women is caused in part by the desire to assert emotional, intellectual, and physical problems without that plastic covering of reticence and euphemism which was demanded by an earlier day. I remember Auden mentioning, in a poem which catalogs the sins for which men may or may not be forgiven, the assumption that ". . . 'Woman is naturally pure/Since she has no moustache,' . . ."

There have been some harsh descriptions of writers as such. Kenneth Rexroth, always a fast man with a sharp word, paints a fairly gruesome picture in *American Poetry in the Twentieth Century*:

> By and large, writers are not very nice people. Most of them are quarrelsome, vindictive, malicious. There are too many piglets, and too little swill in the trough, so there is a good deal of squealing and backbiting. American writers have a fixed idea that they are not welcome in their society and this makes them arrogant.[6]

However much this seems exaggerated, or indeed distorted, no writer would deny its kernel of truth. And if most of the best of the women poets seem curiously uninfected with the virus, it may be cynically argued that until fairly recently the trough was off limits, and they had formed a habit of doing without it. Yet I think it cause for pride that most of the good poetry being written by women has a largeness, a lack of pettiness, a reaching over barriers. To believe that the poetry of women has an especial quality is simply another way of saying that the feminine ethos has its own unique and pervasive quality to offer to the art of poetry.

The making of comparisons, of ranking, of first, second, and thirding of poets, is a second-rate occupation. When George Garrett was here recently, he told me something that is beautifully relevant to this. Some members of an audience who were hostile to W. H. Auden and were sitting on the front row at his lecture asked him, in a provocative manner, whom he considered the five top poets now writing. George said that Mr. Auden bent over, peering formidably down at them, and said, "Poetry isn't —[pause]—a horse race, you know." All too often it is treated as though it were. The issue is not how many women poets will "make it," or in what order of win, place, or show. The core of the matter is the poetry; that it be written, by man or woman; that it be recognized and welcomed.

If, in the 17th and 18th centuries, it was difficult for any woman poet fully to realize her talent, for the woman who was black the difficulty approximated an impossibility. No one can estimate what poetic creativity was smothered under the weight of forced illiteracy, isolation, and the sense of hopelessness. Someone like the distinguished black woman Sojourner Truth (of whom Edmund Wilson writes in *Patriotic Gore,* and who was the heroine of a play of that name by Katherine Garrison Chapin, which ran for many weeks in Harlem) found her outlet in preaching. She was musical and eloquent; inevitably she functioned in the ways open to her, as singer, as evangelist. But at last the poetry of black women is beginning to come into its own.

Can one say that now, in this period roughly coinciding with the end of Marianne Moore's career, there is a definite shape, a direction, an overriding pattern, as legacy in the work of American women poets? Definitely, one cannot.

Sylvia Plath's tragic, inward-turned work; Elizabeth Bishop's and May Swenson's marvelous observation and justice; Louise Bogan's real majesty; Isabella Gardner's highly charged and witty work, with its kinship to Millay; Josephine Miles' and Adrienne Rich's socially oriented work; Anne Sexton's passionate and dramatic self-analysis; June Jordan's or Nikki Giovanni's racial concern; Julia Randall's lyric and metaphysical radiance; Carolyn Kizer's cool, satiric, and highly feminine work—all have little to indicate to us of any future "trend." Interestingly enough, there does not seem to have been a great deal of acute interest in the more far-out forms of technical innovation among the majority of these poets. Never for a minute did they feel that the rupturing of form and structure alone could produce originality; nor did they lose sight of the fact that shock, and the recognition of its validity, come about organically, within the poem.

There is here freedom from the restriction of imposed assumptions. These poets have rejected limitation of subject matter, of vocabulary, of viewpoint. Little of their work is cast in traditional form; rather, form is beautifully responsive to the needs of the individual poem. It is, much of it, distinguished poetry, and in my opinion it holds its own in quality, if not in quantity, with poetry now being written by American men. But what a meaningless comparison, basically, that is. Once the poem is released, how little the poet owns it, or, indeed, matters to the poem. The poem has always been injured by the poet. Never, by man or woman, has it been fully released to its potential. Christopher Marlowe spoke for every poet when he wrote long ago in "Tamburlaine the Great" (and this is my favorite statement of what happens to a poem between its conception and its execution):

> If all the pens that ever poets held
> Had fed the feeling of their masters' thoughts,
> And every sweetness that inspir'd their hearts,
> Their minds, and muses on admired themes;
> If all the heavenly quintessence they still
> From their immortal flowers of poesy,
> Wherein, as in a mirror, we perceive
> The highest reaches of a human wit;
> If these had made one poem's period,
> And all combin'd in beauty's worthiness,
> Yet should there hover in their restless heads
> One thought, one grace, one wonder, at the least,
> Which into words no virtue can digest.

Always, the struggle is to help the poem release itself from the things it cannot, in various stages, do without: publishers, editors, critics, funds, sponsors. Always the effort must be to shift the emphasis back to where it belongs, to the poem, which, though injured and subjected to the thousand ills that print is heir to, must escape and survive.

I have been speaking tonight as a poet and a woman. I would like to end by reading a poem about that freedom of the poem itself from being anyone's possession, about that marvelous thing, escaped, which, since it belongs to no one, speaks to its own. That is what is left in the end.

The Poem Itself

From the ripe silence it exploded silently.
When the bright debris subsided
it was there.

Invisible, inaudible; only
the inky shapes betrayed it.
Betrayed, is the word.

Thence it moved into squalor,
a royal virgin in a brothel,
improbably whole.

It had its followers, pimps, even
its lovers. The man responsible
died, eventually.

When the dust of his brain left the bones
the bond snapped. It escaped to itself.
It no longer answered.

On the shelf, by the clock's tick, in the black
stacks of midnight: it is. A moon
to all its tides.

Notes

[1] Mrs. [Sarah S.] Ellis, *The Family Monitor and Domestic Guide* (New York, H. G. Langley, 1844), quoted in Ann Gabhart and Elizabeth Broun, "Old Mistresses: Women Artists of the Past," *The Bulletin of The Walters Art Gallery,* 24(April 1972).

[2] Kenneth Silverman, ed., *Colonial American Poetry* (New York, Hafner Publishing Company, Inc., 1968), p. 4.

[3] Ibid., p. 7.

[4] These three Dickinson poems are taken from *The Complete Poems of Emily Dickinson,* ed., Thomas H. Johnson (Boston, Little, Brown and Company, 1960).

[5] Josephine Jacobsen and William R. Mueller, *The Testament of Samuel Beckett* (New York, Hill and Wang, 1964), p. 35, 38.

[6] Kenneth Rexroth, *American Poetry in the Twentieth Century* (New York, Herder and Herder, 1971), p. 84.

Other Publications on Literature Issued by the Library of Congress

These publications, based on lectures presented at the Library of Congress, may be purchased from the Superintendent of Documents, Government Printing Office, Washington, D.C. 20402. When ordering, please provide the title, date, and identifying number, and enclose payment.

The Art of History; Two Lectures. 1967. 38 p. (LC 29.9:N41) 30 cents.
The Old History and the New, by Allan Nevins. Biography, History, and the Writing of Books, by Catherine Drinker Bowen.

Carl Sandburg, by Mark Van Doren. With a bibliography of Sandburg materials in the collections of the Library of Congress. 1969. 83 p. (LC 29.9:V28) 50 cents.

Chaos and Control in Poetry; a Lecture, by Stephen Spender. 1966. 14 p. (LC 29.9:SP3/2) 15 cents.

Louise Bogan: A Woman's Words, by William Jay Smith. With a bibliography. 1971. 81 p. (LC 1.14:Sm6) 45 cents.

Metaphor as Pure Adventure. A lecture by James Dickey. 1968. 20 p. (LC 1.14:D55/2) 25 cents.

National Poetry Festival, Held in the Library of Congress, October 22-24, 1962: Proceedings. 1964. 367 p. (LC 2.2:P75/6) $1.50.

Questions to an Artist Who Is Also an Author; a Conversation Between Maurice Sendak and Virginia Haviland. 1972. 18 p. (LC 1.17/A:AR 78) 30 cents.
Reprinted from the October 1971 *Quarterly Journal of the Library of Congress,* v. 28, no. 4.

Randall Jarrell, by Karl Shapiro. With a bibliography of Jarrell materials in the collections of the Library of Congress. 1967. 47 p. (LC 29.9:Sh2) 25 cents.

Robert Frost: A Backward Look, by Louis Untermeyer. With a selective bibliography. 1964. 40 p. (LC 29.9:Un8) 30 cents.

Saint-John Perse: Praise and Presence, by Pierre Emmanuel. With a bibliography. 1971. 82 p. (LC 29.9:P43) 45 cents.

Spinning the Crystal Ball; Some Guesses at the Future of American Poetry, by James Dickey. 1967. 22 p. (LC 1.14:D55) 15 cents.

The Translation of Poetry. Address [by Allen Tate] and panel discussion presented at the International Poetry Festival held at the Library of Congress, April 13-15, 1970. 1972. 40 p. (LC 29.9:T18) 30 cents.

Walt Whitman: Man, Poet, Philosopher. 1955, reissued 1969. 53 p. (LC 29.2:W59/2) 25 cents.

The Man, by Gay Wilson Allen. The Poet, by Mark Van Doren. The Philosopher, by David Daiches.

☆ U.S. GOVERNMENT PRINTING OFFICE: 1973 O—479-930